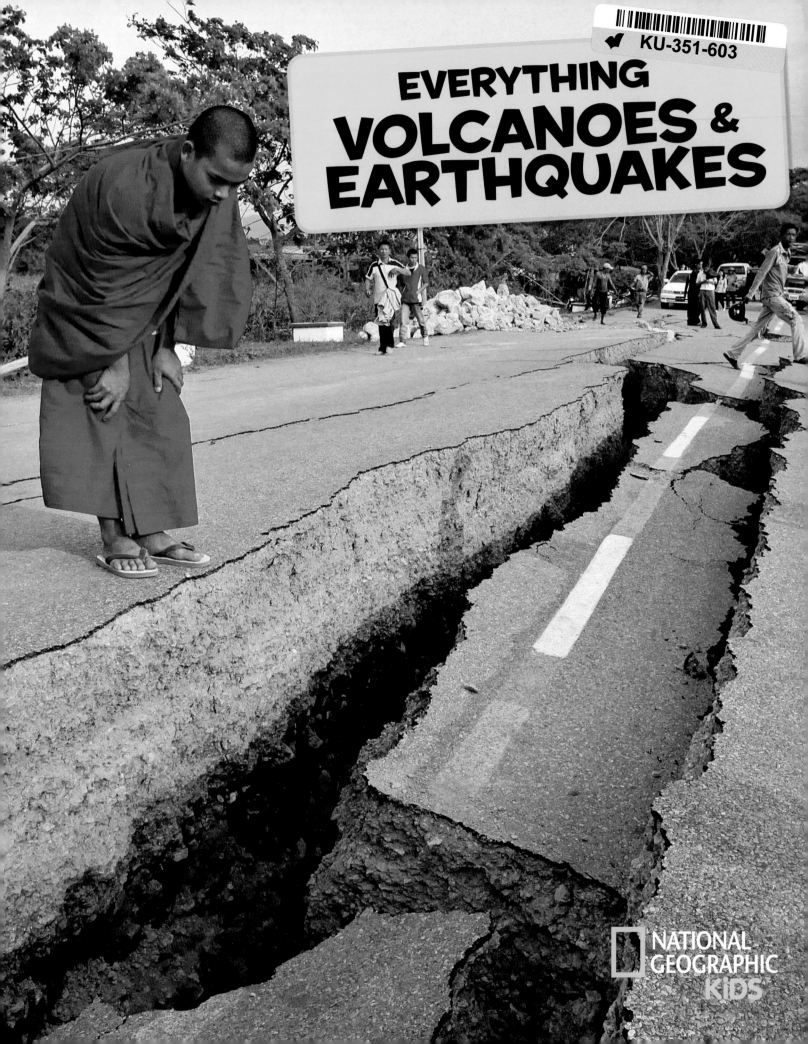

EVERYTHING
VOLCANOES &
EARTHQUAKES

NATIONAL GEOGRAPHIC KiDS

EVERYTHING
VOLCANOES &
EARTHQUAKES

BY KATHY FURGANG

With National Geographic Explorer CARSTEN PETER

CONTENTS

Lava flows into the ocean at Kaula-Kona, Hawaii, U.S.A., at sunrise.

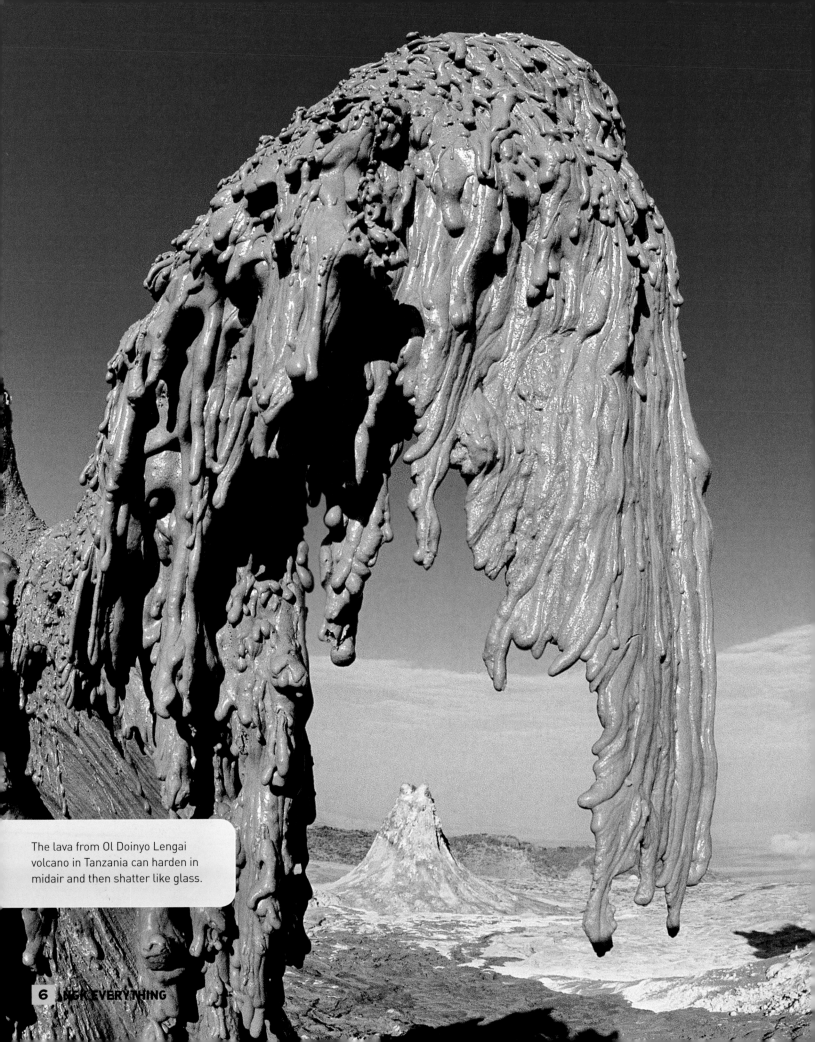

The lava from Ol Doinyo Lengai volcano in Tanzania can harden in midair and then shatter like glass.

INTRODUCTION

PLANET EARTH IS FULL OF **ACTION. ON ANY GIVEN DAY, EARTHQUAKES** shake the ground and split the surface with deep gashes. Volcanic mountains spew rock and thick ash into the air. Fiery-hot rivers of lava flow, then gradually cool to form new landmasses. Even the ocean floor changes constantly. Lava oozes from underwater volcanoes—geologists have identified more than 5,000 of them! Many of these rise over time to break the surface and form islands. Then wind and pounding waves take over, shaping each new landform.

To understand this changing landscape, you have to go back around 5 billion years to when the planet first formed. No time machine? Then, stay right here and hang on for a wild ride as we scale the slopes of an active volcano and shake, rattle and roll with a mighty quake. Let's discover EVERYTHING about volcanoes and earthquakes!

EXPLORER'S CORNER

Hi! I'm Carsten Peter.

I'm a photographer who loves to take pictures of places where no one else can go. My mission takes me to some of the scariest places on Earth: volcanoes, toxic and superheated caves, turbulent lava lakes. These aren't exactly places where my smartphone camera works. So one of the challenges I face, especially when I'm working for National Geographic, is to create special techniques to capture the shots I want. So get ready. Just this once, I'm going to take you with me.

The constant shifting and shaking of Earth's layers builds mountains and moves continents, shaping the surface of the planet. When these natural forces get rough, earthquakes rumble and volcanoes erupt, like Mount Bromo in Indonesia, pictured here.

WHEN EARTH CRACKS UP

WHAT IS A VOLCANO?

IT'S SERIOUSLY

HOT 6,437 KILOMETRES (4,000 MILES) DOWN AT THE CENTRE OF THE EARTH.

The temperature there ranges from 5000 to 7000°C (9032°F to 12,632°F). That kind of heat melts rock into liquid, or molten, form. Sometimes molten rock gushes up and bursts through an opening in Earth's surface—a volcano—in a fiery flow of lava. Sometimes a volcano takes the shape of a mountain. Sometimes it even forms underwater.

MAGMA AND LAVA

Magma is molten rock *before* it reaches Earth's surface. Lava is molten rock *after* it reaches the surface. When lava erupts from a volcano, it can be liquid, semiliquid or solid rock, depending on its temperature. The outer layer of rock can cool within minutes, but thick lava can take years to cool completely.

BUBBLING AND BOILING

Mud pots like these, bubble and steam at the base of some volcanic mountains.

The Karymsky volcano in Russia is the most active volcano in its region. It's been actively erupting for more than 500 years. The volcano produces a fine, powdered rock called ash, which looks like black smoke.

Earthquakes can cause changes—and sometimes tremendous damage—on Earth's surface. Earthquakes can rip apart bridges, roads and buildings (left).

WHAT IS AN EARTHQUAKE?

This crack in the ground (above) in Chile, in South America, was caused by aftershocks that rocked the area a month after a big earthquake.

THE EARTH'S OUTER CRUST MIGHT SEEM ROCK SOLID, BUT IN FACT IT'S PRETTY thin—and put together like a jigsaw puzzle with many natural cracks and breaks. When the crust shifts suddenly we feel things rumbling around. That's an earthquake.

The biggest pieces of the puzzle are called tectonic plates. There are a few major plates and dozens of smaller ones. The edges where the plates touch are called fault lines. When the plates shift along fault lines, magma can rise to the surface and trigger a volcanic eruption. And where the plates pull apart, slide past each other or crash together, they take what's on the surface for a ground-buckling, earthshaking ride.

Most earthquakes are too small for people to feel. Every year there may be millions of tiny quakes that go undetected or unnoticed. However, some major earthquakes are so devastating that they cause landslides, fires, collapsed buildings and even tidal waves thousands of miles away—events that often result in the loss of human lives.

GIANT JIGSAW PUZZLE

Tectonic plates are always on the move. Most action occurs along the edges where two plates meet.

EXPLOSIVE FACT THERE IS A 100 PERCENT CHANCE THAT THERE WILL BE AN EARTHQUAKE SOMEWHERE ON EARTH TODAY!

EARTH BUILDERS

IT'S TIME FOR **YOUR TRIP TO THE CENTRE OF EARTH.** That's where all the action you see on the surface starts— thousands of miles below your feet. Think of Earth as a hard-boiled egg. Earth's core is the yolk. Around it, like the white part of the egg, is Earth's thick mantle. And the outer crust, where we live, is like the eggshell. The crust cracks and crumbles when heat from the core heats rock in the mantle. That heating creates currents that push and pull at the plates at the surface. The pushing and pulling results in volcanoes and earthquakes. It can also create some awesome, twisted, beautiful landscapes.

Many volcanoes form at the bottom of the ocean. It takes many thousands of eruptions for these volcanoes to build up and become islands above the surface of the ocean. These volcanic islands sit near the Equator in the Indian Ocean.

EXPLOSIVE FACT HALF OF EARTH'S GEOTHERMAL FEATURES (GEYSERS, FUMAROLES, HOT SPRINGS AND MUD POTS) ARE IN YELLOWSTONE NATIONAL PARK IN THE U.S.A.

The **CRUST** includes tectonic plates, landmasses and the oceans. Its thickness varies from 5 to 100 km (3 to 62 miles).

The **MANTLE** is about 2,897 km (1,800 miles) of hot, thick, solid rock.

The **OUTER CORE** is liquid molten lava made mostly of iron and nickel.

The **INNER CORE** is a solid centre also made mostly of iron and nickel.

Himalaya, in India and Tibet

MARVELLOUS MOUNTAINS

Earth's plates bump into each other, pushing the surface upward in places. After a few million years, voila—a mountain range!

HEALTHY SOIL

Volcanic rock makes soil fertile, which helps trees and food crops grow well.

Volcanoes National Park, Rwanda

GUSHING GEYSERS

Geysers are hot springs that erupt, shooting superheated water into the air. Yellowstone National Park in Wyoming and Montana, U.S.A., has more than 300 geysers, including Old Faithful. The famous geyser got its name because it's so predictable: It erupts every 60 to 110 minutes. What's heating up all that water? The park sits on top of a supervolcano —one that could blast out more than one thousand billion tons of pumice and ash when it erupts. Look out!

COLOSSAL QUAKES

THROUGHOUT HISTORY, VOLCANOES AND EARTHQUAKES HAVE CAUSED GREAT HARDSHIP FOR PEOPLE all around the world. Even though today's scientists can monitor Earth's movements, they still have no reliable way of predicting exactly when a volcano will erupt or an earthquake will strike. That makes preparing for disaster challenging. Earth's tremors and eruptions sometimes catch people by surprise—the result may be a staggering loss of life and damage to property costing billions of pounds. These are some of the biggest blasts from the past.

QUAKE!

Port-au-Prince, Haiti, 2010

On the 12th of January 2010, a huge earthquake rocked Port-au-Prince, the capital and largest city of Haiti. The quake killed more than 200,000 people and left some 1.5 million others homeless. The quake also damaged a main port and an airport. Dangerous aftershocks rattled the city for months.

QUAKE!

San Francisco, U.S.A., 1906

The 1906 earthquake in San Francisco, California, lasted almost an entire minute, which is a long time when the ground is heaving violently. The earthquake, along with fires that raged for three days, destroyed three-quarters of the city. People as far away as central Nevada—483 km (300 miles) away—felt the shaking.

QUAKE!

Pakistan, 2005

The epicentre of the earthquake was in the Kashmir region of Pakistan on 8th of October 2005. With a magnitude of 7.6, tremors were felt nearby in Afghanistan, southwest China and Tajikistan. More than 80,000 people lost their lives and four million were left homeless. There was widespread destruction and damage to buildings. The area is one of the most active for earthquakes in the world.

ERUPTION!

Mount Vesuvius

In AD 79, Italy's Mount Vesuvius erupted for 24 hours, burying the nearby cities of Pompeii and Herculaneum in ash. Centuries later, archaeologists uncovered the buried cities. They learned that in some places falling ash had piled up as high as 2.7 m (9 feet), blocking doorways and crushing roofs.

It's impossible to know how many died, but the remains of about 2,000 people have been found in excavations at Pompeii. The bodies had decayed, but ash had combined with moisture and moulded around them. Scientists poured plaster into some of the solidified ash moulds. The resulting plaster casts revealed people clutching jewellery and belongings or hugging each other in their final moments.

Scientists agree that Vesuvius is overdue for another major eruption. Today, one million people live in Naples, Italy, much too close for comfort.

Plaster casts of Pompeii victims

EXPLORER'S CORNER

We know that lots of tiny earthquakes happen every day, and no one even notices. We don't expect to feel a quake unless we live near a major fault line. But sometimes there's a surprise. In the summer of 2011, my colleagues at the Washington, D.C., headquarters of the National Geographic Society were rattled by a 5.8 magnitude quake that sent them running, very confused, from their offices. The quake's epicentre was almost a hundred and sixty kilometres (100 miles) away in Virginia! No deaths or serious damage were reported anywhere, but there was definitely a lot of texting and tweeting going on.

EXPLOSIVE FACT ARCHAEOLOGISTS FOUND LOAVES OF BREAD STILL SITTING IN AN OVEN IN POMPEII. THE BREAD HAD TURNED TO STONE, PRESERVED IN VOLCANIC ASH!

CHAIN REACTIONS

VOLCANOES AND EARTHQUAKES

LET LOOSE FEARSOME FORCES.

They can cause tremors that set off a chain reaction of movement in water, on land or in snow.

AVALANCHE

An earthquake can shake a snow-topped mountain—even many miles away from the epicentre. Snowpack gets dislodged and races down slopes in an avalanche, burying whatever is in its path and slamming into the valley below.

The tsunami that followed a massive earthquake in Japan in March 2011 deposited this ship on top of a hotel.

TSUNAMI

A tsunami is a giant wave that begins beneath the surface of the ocean. It radiates out from an undersea earthquake, landslide or large volcanic eruption. A tsunami can produce waves 15–30 metres (50–100 feet) tall that travel at more than 724 kilometres (450 miles) an hour. If one of these towering walls of water reaches land, carrying tons of debris along with it, it can cause massive destruction. Tsunamis lift and toss cars, houses and even huge ships as if they were toys.

Damage from an aftershock in Christchurch, South Island, New Zealand in 2011.

An avalanche races down a 2,135 metre (7,000 foot) chute on Pik Kommunizma, Tajikistan.

Heavy rains caused volcanic mudflows on Mount Merapi in Indonesia.

MUDFLOWS

After a volcanic eruption, rivers of mud and debris can spread over wide areas on land. Even months after an eruption, rainwater can combine with the mud and cause further destruction.

AFTERSHOCKS

An earthquake may be strong enough to rattle a town and cause plenty of damage. Afterward, as the ground settles, smaller quakes called aftershocks can occur. These can be just as dangerous as the initial earthquake, causing more severe damage.

EXPLOSIVE FACT THERE ARE ABOUT HALF A MILLION DETECTABLE EARTHQUAKES IN THE WORLD EACH YEAR.

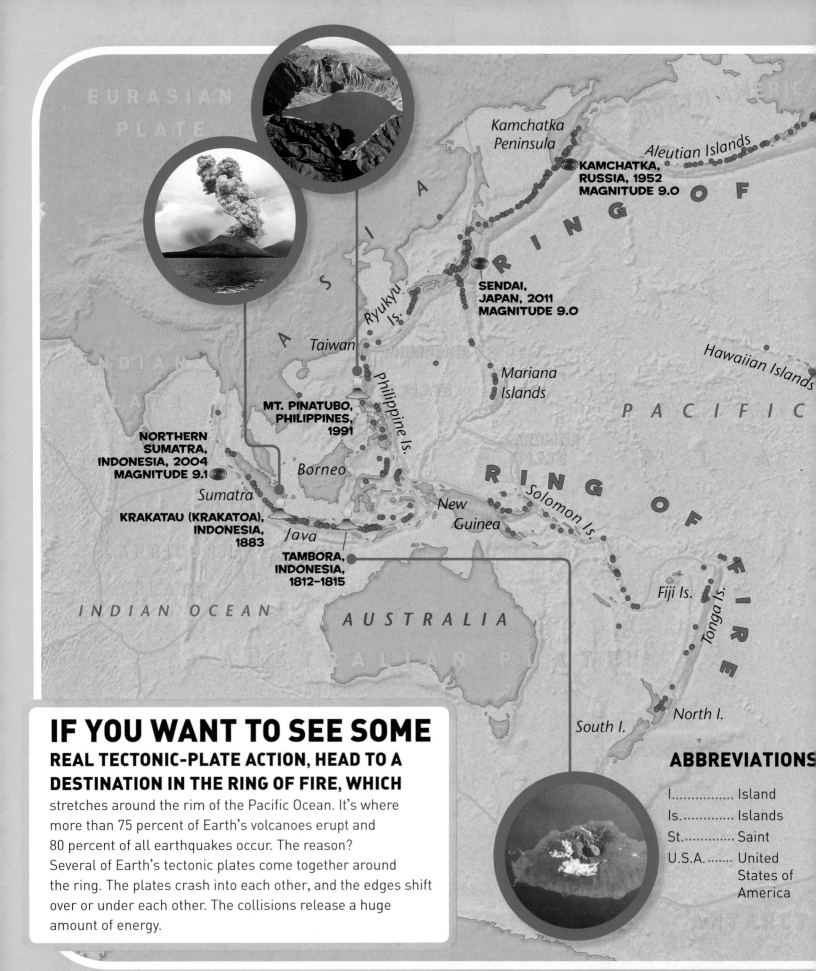

EURASIAN PLATE

Kamchatka Peninsula

Aleutian Islands

⊚ **KAMCHATKA, RUSSIA, 1952 MAGNITUDE 9.0**

R I N G   O F

A S I A

Ryukyu Is.

Taiwan

🌀 **SENDAI, JAPAN, 2011 MAGNITUDE 9.0**

PHILIPPINE PLATE

Mariana Islands

Hawaiian Islands

P A C I F I C

MT. PINATUBO, PHILIPPINES, 1991

Philippine Is.

CAROLINE PLATE

P L A T E

NORTHERN SUMATRA, INDONESIA, 2004 MAGNITUDE 9.1 ⊚

Borneo

R I N G

Solomon Is.

O F

Sumatra

KRAKATAU (KRAKATOA), INDONESIA, 1883

Java

New Guinea

F I R E

TAMBORA, INDONESIA, 1812–1815

CAPRICORN PLATE

Fiji Is.

Tonga Is.

INDIAN OCEAN

A U S T R A L I A

AUSTRALIAN PLATE

South I.

North I.

IF YOU WANT TO SEE SOME

REAL TECTONIC-PLATE ACTION, HEAD TO A DESTINATION IN THE RING OF FIRE, WHICH stretches around the rim of the Pacific Ocean. It's where more than 75 percent of Earth's volcanoes erupt and 80 percent of all earthquakes occur. The reason? Several of Earth's tectonic plates come together around the ring. The plates crash into each other, and the edges shift over or under each other. The collisions release a huge amount of energy.

ABBREVIATIONS

I	Island
Is.	Islands
St.	Saint
U.S.A.	United States of America

ANTARCTICA

RING OF FIRE

NCE WILLIAM
UND,
S.A., 1964
AGNITUDE 9.2

AN DE FUCA
PLATE

MOUNT ST. HELENS,
U.S.A., 1980

NORTH

NORTH AMERICAN PLATE

AMERICA

EL CHICHÓN,
MEXICO,
1982

CARIBBEAN PLATE

RING

COCOS
PLATE

OF

Galápagos
Islands

NAZCA

PLATE

SOUTH

AMERICA

SOUTH

AMERICAN

PLATE

ATLANTIC OCEAN

FIRE

TEMUCO-VALDIVIA,
CHILE, 1960
MAGNITUDE 9.5

SCOTIA PLATE

MAP KEY

- **Strongest earthquakes since 1900**
- **Largest volcanic eruptions in modern history**
- Selected volcano
- Tectonic plate boundary

ANTARCTICA

0 ——— km ——— 2000

0 ——— mi ——— 2000

Volcanologists study the lava spewing from Mount Etna, in Sicily, Italy. The volcano is in an almost constant state of activity and is one of the most active volcanoes in the world.

2
VOLCANO POWER

A HOT TOPIC

WHAT GOES ON INSIDE

A STEAMING, BREWING VOLCANO? If you could look inside a volcano, you'd see something that looks like a long pipe, called a conduit. It leads from inside the magma chamber under the crust up to a vent, or opening, at the top of the mountain. Some conduits have branches that shoot off to the side, called fissures.

When pressure builds from gases inside the volcano, the gases must find an escape, and they head up toward the surface! An eruption occurs when lava, gases, ash, and rocks explode out of the vent.

CRATER

VENT

CONDUIT

FISSURE

MAGMA CHAMBER

HARDENED LAVA AND ASH LAYERS

TYPES OF VOLCANOES

CINDER CONE VOLCANO
Eve's Cone, Canada

Cinder cone volcanoes look like an upside-down ice-cream cone. They spew out cinder and hot ash. Some of these volcanoes smoke and erupt for years at a time.

COMPOSITE VOLCANO
Licancábur, Chile

Composite volcanoes, or stratovolcanoes, form as lava, ash and cinder from previous eruptions harden and build up over time. These volcanoes spit out pyroclastic flows, or thick explosions of hot ash that travel at hundreds of miles (km) an hour.

SHIELD VOLCANO
Mauna Loa, Hawaii, U.S.A.

The gentle, broad slopes of a shield volcano look like an ancient warrior's shield. Its eruptions are often slower. Lava splatters and bubbles rather than shooting forcefully into the air.

LAVA DOME VOLCANO
Puy de Dôme, France

Dome volcanoes have steep sides. Hardened lava often plugs the vent at the top of a dome volcano. Pressure builds beneath the surface until the top blows. There has been an observatory on Puy de Dôme since 1876.

HOT SPOTS
Some volcanoes form at hot spots or holes beneath Earth's crust in the middle of a tectonic plate. As lava pushes up through the hole and forms a volcanic island, the plate keeps moving. More volcanoes form as it moves. Some hot spots are big enough to create a chain of volcanic islands, such as the Hawaiian Islands.

COLLAPSE!
An erupting volcano can cause damage to itself! A caldera is a large bowl-like depression caused by the collapse of a magma chamber during an eruption. Crater Lake in Oregon, U.S.A., is a caldera that has filled with rainwater and snowfall.

EXPLOSIVE FACT A LITRE OF VOLCANIC ASH IS TEN TIMES HEAVIER THAN A LITRE OF SNOW!

UNDERWATER ACTION

A deep-water submersible explores the El Bajo Seamount, an underwater point off the coast of Central America.

THE HEAT PRODUCED
AT EARTH'S CORE GIVES RISE

to some mysterious goings-on down deep, where only submarines and ROVs (remotely operated vehicles that are directed underwater by an operator aboard a boat) go. With the help of some high-tech devices, scientists are going to depths of 5,000 metres (16,000 feet) to film, scrape and take samples from the ocean floor. With their help, we're learning a lot about underwater volcanoes.

EXTREME LIFE-FORMS

Tube worms thrive in the heat and consume the bacteria around hydrothermal vents. Specially adapted to the dark, scalding-hot and toxic environment, tube worms can grow to be nearly two and a half metres (eight feet) long.

HYDROTHERMAL VENTS

Hot springs on the ocean floor gush mineral-rich fluids through hydrothermal vents. These vents are formed when plates under the ocean move apart. Seawater seeps into the cracks and is heated by the molten rock beneath.

A black smoker is a blast of water as hot as 400°C (750°F) that shoots out of a hydrothermal vent. The water looks like black smoke because it is full of sulphur.

STINKY GAS

Sulphur from El Hierro, an underwater volcano in the Canary Islands, turned the surrounding waters bright green.

SPREADING SEAFLOOR

Scientists are always tracking plate movements at the bottom of the ocean floor. Underwater volcanic mountain ranges, called mid-ocean ridges, rise up where the edges of plates push together. Meanwhile, slowly but steadily, the continents are spreading apart. The spreading seafloor may be widening Earth's oceans by about 2.5 cm each year.

EXPLOSIVE FACT
MARS HAS A VOLCANO NAMED OLYMPUS MONS THAT IS ABOUT TWO AND A HALF TIMES THE HEIGHT OF MOUNT EVEREST.

SMOKIN' FACTS ABOUT VOLCANOES

WHAT DO YOU CALL SOMEONE WHO CAN'T GET ENOUGH OF VOLCANOES?

A volcanologist. That's a scientist who studies volcanoes and watches their activity sometimes at very close range. Volcanologists learn a lot from studying volcanoes before— as well as after—eruptions. For example, they monitor active and dormant volcanoes for temperature changes and emission of sulphur and other toxic gases. The data they gather provides clues about when a volcano may be ready to blow its top. Their work saves lives. Here are some cool facts about volcanoes that will make you feel like a volcanologist.

A volcanologist wears a protective suit to study volcanoes.

Eyjafjallajökull volcano, Iceland

VOLCANO LIGHTNING

You can see lightning in the middle of a volcanic ash cloud—it sparks when particles collide, creating friction and an electrical charge.

LAVA CAVES

Sometimes a lava flow stops, cools and hollows out, leaving a tunnel which people can walk through.

ACID LAKES

Lakes in volcano craters can contain water so concentrated with gases that it burns through flesh in minutes!

[top photo] Mount St. Helens National Volcanic Monument, Washington, U.S.A. [middle photo] Lake Nyos, Cameroon [bottom photo] Mount Tambora, Indonesia

A YEAR WITHOUT SUMMER

The 1815 volcanic blast on Mount Tambora, in Indonesia, is the largest volcanic eruption in recorded history. Ash and dust spread around the globe, blocking the summer sun and causing a 'volcanic winter'.

EXPLORER'S CORNER

Volcanologists suit up in some pretty high-tech gear when they get up close and personal with the inside of an active volcano—and when I go with them to get shots of their work, so do I. Our suits, coated with aluminum, were first developed by NASA in the 1950s to protect astronauts, but come in handy—like full-body oven gloves—near lakes of molten rock, too! The aluminum helps bounce heat rays off, and layers underneath insulate us in temperatures as high as 260°C (500°F). We need air tanks and breathing apparatus, helmets with special glass lenses, and, of course, special gloves and boots. Even my cameras are custom-made!

THE UPSIDE OF VOLCANOES

VOLCANOES AREN'T ALL BAD NEWS.

They provide many rich resources. Soil made from volcanic material promotes healthy plant life. Geothermal power, which comes from the heat inside the Earth, is a renewable energy source that can power homes and factories. In fact, about 70 percent of Iceland's energy comes from volcanic geothermal power. Volcanoes offer luxurious resources, too. Valuable minerals and precious gems are the work of volcanoes. Mud baths and mineral spas are some of the unique by-products of the natural power of volcanoes.

Ahhhhh! In Iceland's Blue Lagoon, at the base of a geothermal power plant, tourists soak in nature's hot tub, heated by lava fields.

EXPLOSIVE FACT IN JAPAN, SNOW MONKEYS WARM UP IN WINTER BY SOAKING IN VOLCANIC HOT SPRINGS.

MUD MASK
Your skin won't get clean in this bath, but it'll sure look good afterwards! Mineral-rich volcanic mud draws tourists to lots of spas in New Zealand.

BURIED TREASURE
When solid magma spews out of volcanic vents, it sometimes carries kimberlite with it, a rare blue rock that occasionally contains diamonds.

RUB-A-DUB-DUB
Pumice, a volcanic rock, is the lightest rock on Earth. It even floats in water. Many people rub their skin with pumice when they bathe to soften or remove hard skin on elbows and feet.

A PHOTO GALLERY

AWESOME EARTH

THE POWER OF MOTHER NATURE IS SCARY AND AMAZING.

Whether we see them in action or witness the aftermath, earthquakes and volcanoes change the shape of our planet and capture our imagination.

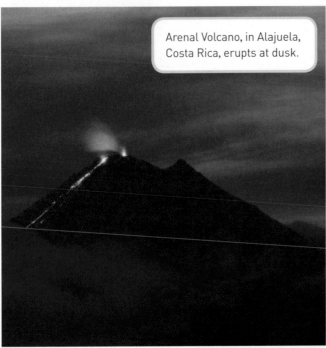

Arenal Volcano, in Alajuela, Costa Rica, erupts at dusk.

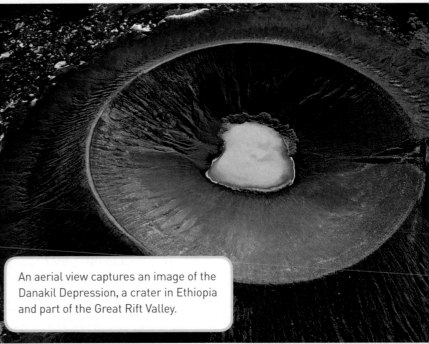

An aerial view captures an image of the Danakil Depression, a crater in Ethiopia and part of the Great Rift Valley.

Giant's Causeway in Northern Ireland contains basalt columns created by an ancient eruption.

A fracture in the Earth lies next to volcanic cones in Great Rift Valley, Djibouti, in Africa.

Lava flows from Fimmvorouhals volcano in Iceland.

A snapshot of Russia's Kamchatka Peninsula, taken from space, shows four volcanoes erupting at once.

Lava fountains bubble inside the crater of Mount Etna in Sicily, Italy.

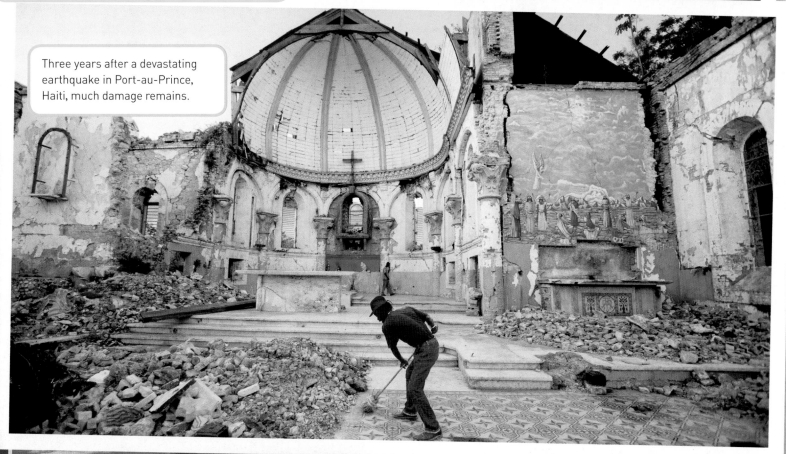

Three years after a devastating earthquake in Port-au-Prince, Haiti, much damage remains.

Tofua Island, Tonga, has a freshwater lake inside the volcano's caldera.

Mount Hood in Oregon, U.S.A., is reflected in the waters of Trillium Lake.

Human engineering can be no match for a powerful earthquake. When a strong quake strikes, structures can buckle and crumble in an instant. In 1995, an earthquake destroyed this highway in Osaka, Kobe, Japan.

③ SHAKE, RATTLE & ROLL

KNOW YOUR QUAKES

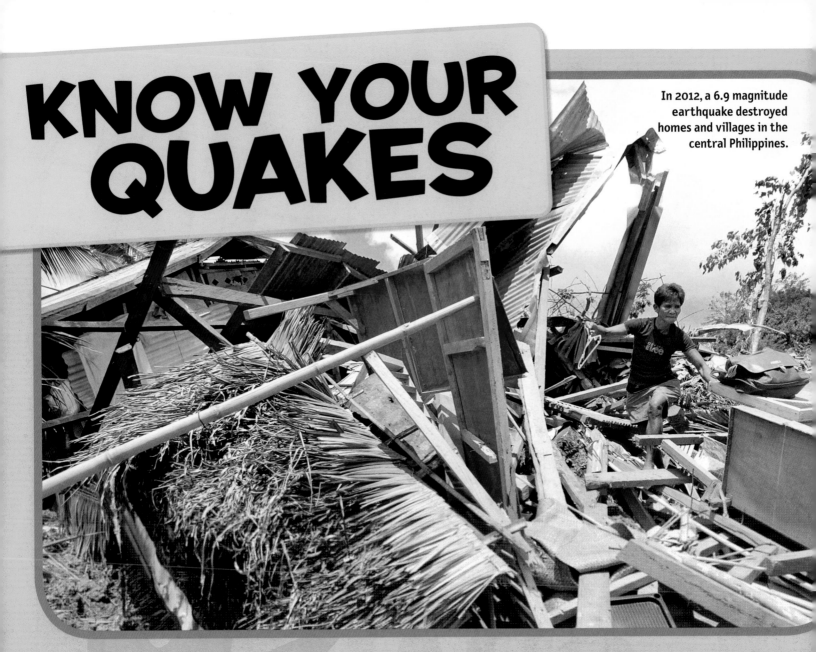

In 2012, a 6.9 magnitude earthquake destroyed homes and villages in the central Philippines.

THE STRONGEST EARTHQUAKE IN THE U.K. WAS 6.1. IT WAS IN THE NORTH SEA IN 1931. CHILE HAD THE WORLD'S STRONGEST QUAKE WITH 9.5 IN 1960

THE SPOT WHERE AN EARTHQUAKE RUPTURES IS CALLED ITS EPICENTRE.

Vibrations called seismic waves travel out around the epicentre in circles, like ripples from a rock tossed into a lake. People living hundreds of miles from the epicentre can sometimes feel the Earth shudder beneath their feet.

People have tried to predict earthquakes for thousands of years. Knowing when an earthquake will happen can help people prepare for disaster. Scientists are still developing tools to measure the power, duration and direction of an earthquake because these are clues to what might happen in the future.

MOMENT MAGNITUDE SCALE

The moment magnitude scale measures the size of an earthquake by the amount of energy it releases. Developed in the 1970s by Thomas Hanks and Hiroo Kanamori, the scale is a successor to the Richter scale. Here's how to rate a quake:

10+ has not been recorded

9 severe—occurs once every 5 to 20 years

8 serious damage over a large area

7 serious damage to buildings and structures

6 strong enough to be destructive

5 moderate damage over a small area

4 minor damage—occurs daily around the world

3 often felt but rarely causes damage

2 (or less) not usually felt, but recorded by seismographs

TRACKING EARTHQUAKES

A seismograph can measure and record the strength of the seismic waves that move away from the quake's epicentre. It detects the smallest changes in Earth's movements. The device converts the movements into electronic signals that are recorded by a computer. Scientists combine the data from several seismographs to locate the quake's epicentre and figure out how deep and strong the quake is.

ANCIENT EARTHQUAKE DETECTOR

Zhang Hen was a Chinese inventor who lived from AD 78–139. Historians credit him with constructing the world's first seismometer, shown here. When the ground shook, a ball fell from the dragon's head into a toad-shaped container below. The device showed the direction of the quake's epicentre.

By the Numbers

500,000 quakes are detected around the globe each year.

100,000 quakes are strong enough to be felt by people each year.

100 quakes are strong enough to cause some damage each year.

3 quakes are strong enough to cause serious damage over large areas each year.

CAN ANIMALS PREDICT EARTHQUAKES?

ARE ANIMALS TRYING TO TELL US SOMETHING WHEN THEY SEEM TO GO WILD FOR NO REASON?

It turns out that animals may be more sensitive to vibrations and chemical changes in rocks and air than humans are. As far back as 373 BC, people reported seeing rats, snakes and weasels fleeing a city in Greece just days before a devastating earthquake.

In 1975, hibernating snakes slithered out of their winter burrows and hightailed it out of Haicheng, China. One month later a large earthquake shook the city. Even elephants are tuned in to quakes. Just hours before a tremendous tsunami hit Thailand in 2004, anxious elephants ran to higher ground. Since scientists can't create earthquakes in a lab, it's difficult to prove that animals are accurate predictors of natural disasters. Even so, it probably makes sense to pay attention to animals when they start acting strangely.

EXPLOSIVE FACT IN 1989 A GEOLOGIST PREDICTED THE SAN FRANCICO EARTHQUAKE A WEEK BEFORE IT OCCURRED WHEN HE NOTICED A LARGE NUMBER OF MISSING PET NOTICES IN THE LOCAL CLASSIFIED ADS.

SNAKE ALERT

Three days before Mount Pelée erupted on the island of Martinique in 1902, dozens of pit vipers appeared in the town of St. Pierre, killing some 50 people and 200 animals with their venomous bites. Centipedes and ants also left their mountain homes before Pelée blew.

NO EGGS TODAY

Farmers are tuned in to their chickens, and the birds may be tuned in to earthquake warning signs. Over the years, many farmers have reported that chickens stop laying eggs before large earthquakes.

Asian elephants

EXPLORER'S CORNER

Scientists see evidence of fault movement in some unlikely places. California's San Andreas Fault (background image) runs through forests of redwoods (inset), the planet's tallest trees. Some trunks show distinct zigzags as they reach toward the sky. And deep in one forest stands a stump split down the middle by an earthquake. It's the size of a small living room, and the gap in the middle, right in line with the fault, is big enough for a man to climb in.

EXPLOSIVE FACT IN THE U.S.A. THE MOVEMENTS OF PLATES ALONG CALIFORNIA'S SAN ANDREAS FAULT ARE SLOWLY MOVING LOS ANGELES AND SAN FRANCISCO CLOSER TOGETHER. THEY COULD BE NEIGHBOURS IN SEVERAL MILLION YEARS.

LIVING ON THE FAULT LINE

TSUNAMI EVACUATION ROUTE

EARTHQUAKES CAN MAKE LIFE DIFFICULT

for months and even years after they occur. A massive quake can destroy roads, bridges and airport runways. When this happens, people can't get the food or supplies they need. However, with the right training and advance planning, people can survive big jolts safely.

TSUNAMI WARNINGS

When earthquakes occur at the bottom of the ocean, the aftershocks reach far and wide away from the epicentre. Many coastal cities have tsunami warning systems that set off alarms warning residents to flee coastal areas. The alarms are triggered by signals from special buoys out at sea that sense changes in sea level after an underwater earthquake. Coastal regions round the Pacific Ocean and parts of the Indian Ocean are particularly in danger from tsunamis.

HERE WE GO AGAIN

The 2011 earthquake in Japan hit 9.0 on the magnitude scale and then produced more than 400 aftershock quakes with a magnitude of at least 5 or greater! There was a further aftershock of 7.4 in November 2016.

LOOK TO THE WATER

Aftershocks can make waves in a pond or swimming pool roll back and forth. The phenomenon is called a *seiche* (pronounced saysh) or standing wave.

ALWAYS LEARNING

Scientists at the Oregon State University Wave Research Laboratory in Oregon, U.S.A., use the wave machine basin to simulate the powerful waves made by a tsunami. Recently, the Dutch have built the Delta Flume, a concrete trough 274 metres (900 feet) in length. Pistons move 9 092 000 litres (2 million gallons) of water back and forth to simulate waves up 4.5 metres (15 feet) high. Both these wave machine help us better understand beach erosion and coastal flooding.

BRACE YOURSELF

SAN FRANCISCO'S TRANSAMERICA PYRAMID HAS A 16-METRE-DEEP (52 FT) FOUNDATION THAT CAN SHIFT WITH THE MOTION OF AN EARTHQUAKE.

MILLIONS OF PEOPLE LIVE
IN AREAS THAT ARE PRONE TO EARTHQUAKES.

For them, learning how to stay safe during a quake is a necessity. They need to be in specially designed buildings and protected from falling objects and shattering glass.

A HELPING HAND

It takes many volunteers to help people after a natural disaster. Rescuing survivors from the rubble is difficult and dangerous. Organisations such as the Red Cross and other 'first responders' help save countless lives. When homes are destroyed, organisations and volunteers also help people find shelters with the necessary food, water and supplies.

LIKE THE REAL THING

Earthquake simulators are close to the real thing. They produce effects in a van or room that are similar to quakes with magnitudes of 3 to 8. People can learn safety measures by using simulators to practise avoiding injuries. Architects and engineers also learn good design principles with these tools.

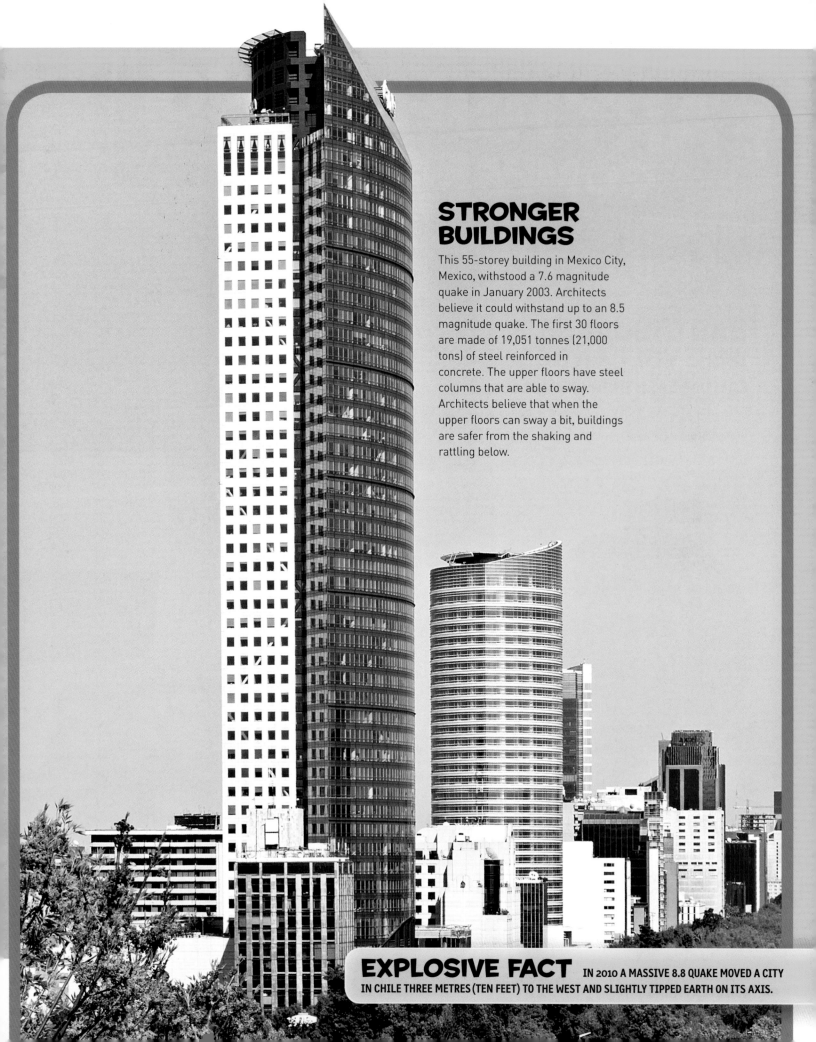

STRONGER BUILDINGS

This 55-storey building in Mexico City, Mexico, withstood a 7.6 magnitude quake in January 2003. Architects believe it could withstand up to an 8.5 magnitude quake. The first 30 floors are made of 19,051 tonnes (21,000 tons) of steel reinforced in concrete. The upper floors have steel columns that are able to sway. Architects believe that when the upper floors can sway a bit, buildings are safer from the shaking and rattling below.

EXPLOSIVE FACT IN 2010 A MASSIVE 8.8 QUAKE MOVED A CITY IN CHILE THREE METRES (TEN FEET) TO THE WEST AND SLIGHTLY TIPPED EARTH ON ITS AXIS.

EARTHSHAKING COMPARISONS

HOW HOT? HOW MUCH? HOW FAST?

EARTHQUAKES AND VOLCANOES CAN UNLEASH UNBELIEVABLE

amounts of force and energy. Take a look at how Earth's awesome action measures up to things you're familiar with.

KRAKATAU, 1883

This volcanic eruption in Indonesia released energy equal to 13,000 times the nuclear yield of the bomb that hit Hiroshima in World War II.

HOW HOT IS LAVA?

The average temperature of lava is about 1100°C (2000°F). That's four times hotter than the hottest setting of a kitchen oven!

EXPLOSIVE FACT PEOPLE HEARD THE BLAST FROM THE 1883 ERUPTION OF KRAKATAU SOME 4,653 KILOMETRES (2,900 MILES) AWAY.

HOW FAST DOES A TSUNAMI TRAVEL?

In deep ocean waters, a tsunami moves as fast as an aeroplane.

HOW FAST DOES A TECTONIC PLATE MOVE?

Tectonic plates move at an average of 2.5 cm (one inch) every year. Your hair grows about six times faster than that!

HOW MUCH ENERGY DOES AN EARTHQUAKE RELEASE?

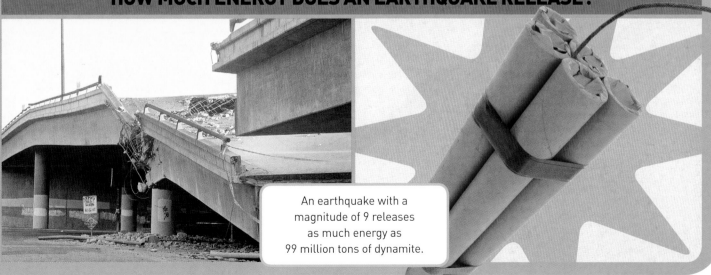

An earthquake with a magnitude of 9 releases as much energy as 99 million tons of dynamite.

Volcanoes, like this one in Indonesia, have become popular tourist destinations for people looking for 'adventure travel'.

HAVE A BLAST!

THE STUFF OF LEGENDS

LONG BEFORE

PEOPLE UNDERSTOOD WHAT CAUSED NATURE'S FURY, THEY created legends about fiery volcanoes and Earth's angry tremors. These colourful stories tried to make sense of an unpredictable world. From one generation to the next, the stories were told and retold. Even today, artists, writers and storytellers are inspired by the powers of nature. It's a long tradition.

VULCAN

More than 2,000 years ago, the Romans worshipped Vulcan, the Roman god of fire. They believed that Vulcan controlled destructive fires, especially volcanoes. People prayed to this deity when they wanted to stay safe from fire. To keep the god happy, they built temples to honour him. Vulcan was good at making things, using fire to forge metal objects. He married Venus, the goddess of love and beauty.

PELE, HAWAIIAN GODDESS OF FIRE

Don't anger the Hawaiian goddess Pele! People say she lives in the crater of Kilauea, on the island of Hawaii. She controls the lava and has the ability to destroy anything in her path. Still, some people say she is kind and call her 'She Who Shapes the Sacred Land'. According to legend, Pele can take the form of a beautiful young woman, or an old woman with a white dog.

LAVA LAMP

To make a groovy lava lamp, first you'll need a tall jar.

1 Pour about 15 cm (6 inches) of water into the jar.

2 Add 2/3 cup of vegetable oil.

3 Wait until the oil rises to the top. Then add two drops of red food colouring to the oil.

4 To make your oily 'lava' flow, shake some salt into the jar. Continue adding salt for as long as you want to make the bubbles sink and float in the water. Place the jar in front of a lamp for best results.

WHAT JUST HAPPENED?

Your lava lamp doesn't contain real lava—it just looks like it. Here's how it works. The oil floats on the water because it is less dense. The salt is denser, so it sinks to the bottom, pulling some oil along with it. As the salt dissolves, the oil floats back to the top. Now you have a cool lava flow that won't burn your hands!

Great Heights

9,170 METRES (30,080 feet) is the height of Mauna Loa volcano, which makes up part of Hawaii. It begins below the ocean.

5,895 METRES (19,341 feet) is the height of Kilimanjaro, the tallest mountain in Africa— and also a volcano.

30 KILOMETRES (19 miles) was the height reached by the ash cloud over the volcano Hekla, in Iceland, in a 1947 eruption.

500 METRES (1,640 feet) was the height to which some lava fountains rose in the eruption of Askja, a volcano in Iceland.

THE AMAZING VANISHING CITY

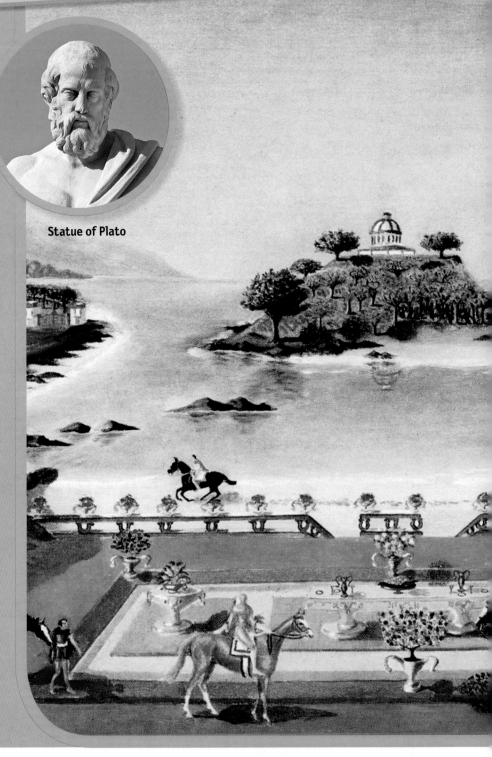

Statue of Plato

YOU MAY HAVE HEARD THE STORY OF THE LOST CITY OF ATLANTIS. IT IS ONE OF THOSE AMAZING

mysteries that historians and scientists continue to debate. Around 360 BC, Greek philosopher Plato wrote about an island that was lost forever under the Atlantic Ocean. It took just one day and one night, he wrote, for the ancient city to be lost to the sea. It was not until the 1800s when someone studied global flood histories and realised that Plato's story may be partly true.

COULD PLATO'S STORY BE TRUE?

Plato described Atlantis as a city built on a hill surrounded by water, with tunnels and canals for ships. Huge fields and farms fed a great civilisation. Plato lived from 427 BC to 347 BC. It turns out that one of the biggest volcanic eruptions since the last ice age happened on the Greek island of Santorini, in about 1620 BC. That huge eruption probably caused the demise of an entire civilisation called the Minoans, and caused the volcano's caldera to sink underwater. This eruption may have sparked the legendary story.

OTHER WILD THEORIES

Not everyone agrees with the theory that Atlantis may have been part of the Greek islands. Other theories suggest that the city was located in Bolivia, near the Andes Mountains. Still others say that the city was near an island off the coast of Florida. The rest of the debaters claim that Central America, the China Sea, or Africa are the real locations of this legendary city.

An artist's concept of the Lost City of Atlantis.

THE WORLD IN YOUR HANDS

Learning about earthquakes and volcanoes can include some hands-on fun. Geologists like to head into the field to get dirty. You, too, can shake some things up, as long as you don't do anything too explosive or dangerous! Here are some activities you can do at home to help experience some of the effects of Earth's rattling, rocking powers.

MAKING MOUNTAINS

1 Place a piece of sugar paper on a table and, down the centre of the paper, draw a mountain range. Name the range, and make some mountains larger than others.

2 Place one hand on either side of the paper. Slowly push your hands toward each other to see how the mountain range rises and changes.

WHAT JUST HAPPENED?

What you're doing with your hands is the same as pushing tectonic plates together, causing the edges to crumple up against each other. Many earthquakes and volcanoes are found along mountain ranges like the one you've drawn. If you were to do this demonstration in real time, you would have to move your hands about 2.5 cm (one inch) a year. That's how slowly Earth's plates really move.

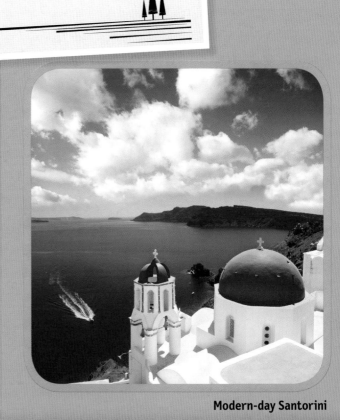

Modern-day Santorini

EXPLOSIVE FACT IN GREEK MYTHOLOGY, POSEIDON, GOD OF THE SEA AND EARTHQUAKES, HAD A SON WHO WAS BORN IN THE CITY OF ATLANTIS.

EARTH SMART

GEOLOGISTS USE MOMENT MAGNITUDE TO MEASURE THE MAGNITUDE of earthquakes, and they use something called the Volcanic Explosivity Index (VEI) to rate volcanoes. The VEI relies on a combination of variables—such as the volume of all lava, ash and rock produced by the eruption. A zero on the scale means the eruption was non-explosive, and an eight means an ash cloud over 50 km (31 miles) high!

YOU RATE IT

Match the earthquake damage to the moment magnitude scale number.

A 1–3 MAGNITUDE

B 4–5 MAGNITUDE

C 6–8 MAGNITUDE

1

2

3

VOLCANO MATCH-UP

TEST YOUR KNOWLEDGE

about the different kinds of volcanoes you've read about in this book. Hopefully this game won't make you blow your top! Match each photo to the correct type of volcano.

A CINDER CONE VOLCANO

. . . .

B SHIELD VOLCANO

. . . .

C COMPOSITE VOLCANO

. . . .

D LAVA DOME

HOT ROCKS

Rocks that start out as hot, molten magma are called igneous rocks. When magma flows up to the surface—where it is called lava—and starts to cool, it forms volcanic rocks. When the magma starts to cool underground, it forms plutonic rocks.

OBSIDIAN

A volcanic glass that cools so quickly that crystals can't form

GRANITE PORPHYRY

A coarse-grained plutonic rock with large crystals of quartz and feldspar

GABBRO

A coarse-grained plutonic rock formed from iron and magnesium-rich magma

PUMICE

An extremely lightweight volcanic rock formed from fast-cooling lava with lots of gas

EXPLOSIVE FACT THE LARGEST MUDFLOW EVER—30 METRES (98 FEET) THICK—BEGAN ON THE TOP OF MOUNT RAINIER IN WASHINGTON STATE, U.S.A.

ANSWERS: A.4, B.1, C.2, D.3

POP CULTURE DISASTERS

MATCH THE
PLACE ON THE LEFT
with the film on the right that's associated with it.

1 Ngauruhoe

This is the youngest of a volcanic trio that rises in the heart of New Zealand's Tongariro National Park. It seems almost magical in the perfect symmetry of its cone.

2 Washington, D.C.

In 2011, an earthquake made the Washington Monument in Washington, D.C., U.S.A., shake and rattle, leaving a crack in the monument. It was just a coincidence that two years earlier a film had come out in which a natural disaster struck Washington, D.C.

3 Mount Etna

This is an active volcano on the east coast of Sicily. It is the tallest active volcano in Europe and one of the most active volcanoes in the world.

CRUST

MANTLE

OUTER CORE

INNER CORE

A Star Wars Episode III: Revenge of the Sith

A volcano starred as a part of the landscape on the planet Mustafar in the 2005 film *Star Wars Episode III: Revenge of the Sith*.
Hint: The camera crew might have enjoyed pasta on location.

B The Lord of the Rings

In J.R.R. Tolkien's *The Lord of the Rings* trilogy, Mount Doom is the volcano where the magical 'ring to rule them all'. with its dark powers, was created—and it's the only place where the ring can be destroyed.
Hint: The trilogy was filmed in a country below the Equator.

C 2012

In the film *2012*, a man fights to save his family from massive earthquakes that throw cities into the ocean, knock down famous landmarks, and threaten to destroy the planet.

WHAT'S DOWN BELOW?

Match each layer of Earth to its description.

A. This is the perfect place to gaze at 2,897 km (1,800 miles) of dense liquid rock.

. . . .

B. It has many kilometres of solid rock, but can still be compared to the skin of an apple.

. . . .

C. Iron and nickel make up this deep layer of Earth.

. . . .

D. Liquid iron and nickel is most of the scenery in this hot zone.

ANSWERS: A: mantle, B: crust, C: inner core, D: outer core

EXPLOSIVE FACT MOUNT SNOWDON IN NORTHERN WALES WAS FORMED BY VOLCANOES AROUND 450 MILLION YEARS AGO. IT IS NOW EXTINCT.

PHOTO FINISH

DON'T JUMP IN *THIS* LAKE!

IT IS 0.4 KM DOWN FROM THE RIM OF

Nyiragongo, a volcano in the centre of Africa. What was I doing there? I was working with scientists who are desperate to learn as much as they can, as fast as they can, about this volcano. Why? Because it's only a matter of time before it erupts, and close to a million people live right by its base. By looking inside to study Nyiragongo's rocks, sample its gases, and watch how it works, scientists hope to answer a big question: When?

After a day of hiking, we reached Nyiragongo's rim, over 3,400 metres (11,000 feet) high. Even up there we could feel the heat of the lava in the lake below, exploding in fiery orange geysers. It was an amazing sight. Pretty terrifying too.

But we had scarier stuff to do. Wearing gas masks and other special equipment (check my Explorer's Corner on page 27), we made our way with ropes down the inner walls of the crater and set up camp on a wide ledge 244 metres (800 feet) down. The air (if you could call it that) was filled with acid and metal particles.

There on the ledge, the scientists set up a field laboratory to measure all the toxic gases. By monitoring the gases and measuring changes in their chemical makeup, they might be able, over time, to find clues about what leads to an eruption. That means they'll need to make regular return visits. Chances are I won't be with them. I made it all the way down to the crater floor, to within feet of the edge of the roiling, bubbling, lava lake. Been there, done that!

Carsten Peter poses in a safe spot during his fieldwork at Nyiragongo.

AFTERWORD

ANIMALS TO THE RESCUE

HUMANS AREN'T THE ONLY
VOLUNTEERS RUSHING TO THE RESCUE AFTER

natural disasters like earthquakes and volcanoes.

Search and rescue dogs train for many specialised tasks, but one of the most important is to sniff both the air and the ground for signs of life. What exactly are they trained to identify? They can smell the microscopic skin cells that humans constantly shed. Dogs travel with firefighters, police, and other special handlers—and save many lives after disasters.

Smaller animals come in handy, too. Would you believe cockroaches with cameras? Absolutely. Six-legged creepy crawlies carry audio and video equipment into places that are too small or too dangerous for rescue dogs. Scientists use low-grade electrical pulses to steer the cockroaches around obstacles and into places where people may be trapped. Rescue crews can then analyse feedback and decide which areas to dig out first, and which areas need to be cleared with extra care.

A cockroach loaded with audio and video equipment is a little bigger than a ten pence piece.

This rescue worker and trained dog are searching for survivors of a massive earthquake and tsunami that hit Japan in March 2011.

Worried that volcanic ash from Iceland's Eyjafjallajökull volcano would damage planes, air travel was stopped for about a week in 2010 in many European countries.

AN INTERACTIVE GLOSSARY

A helicopter hovers over the erupting Kilauea volcano in Hawaii.

PEOPLE WHO STUDY VOLCANOES AND EARTHQUAKES USE THESE WORDS.

Check the glossary to see what each word means, and visit its page numbers to see how the word is used in context. Then test whether your knowledge is a bit shaky or rock solid.

Caldera
(PAGES 22–23)
A large depression in a volcano caused by the collapse of a magma chamber during an eruption.

What forms when a caldera fills with rainwater?
a. quicksand
b. a lake
c. mountains
d. lava

Composite volcano
(PAGES 22–23)
A volcanic mountain formed by hardened layers of lava, ash and cinder from previous eruptions.

What happens to a composite volcano over time?
a. It gets taller.
b. It gets hotter.
c. It is struck by lightning.
d. It erupts more often.

Dormant volcano
(PAGE 26)
A volcano that has not erupted since the last ice age, but is expected to erupt again.

Which word best describes something that is dormant?
a. melted
b. noisy
c. active
d. asleep

Fissure
(PAGES 22–23)
A smaller pipe that shoots off from the side of a volcano's central pipe.

Which analogy best describes a fissure? A fissure is to a volcano as _____.
a. perfume is to air
b. an ice cube is to water
c. a branch is to a tree
d. a bird is to a bush

Geothermal energy
(PAGES 28–29)
Energy that is made from the heat in Earth's interior.

Which of these is a source of geothermal energy?
a. earthquakes
b. volcanoes
c. tsunamis
d. landslides

Hydrothermal vent
(PAGES 24–25)
An opening in the seafloor through which hot, mineral-rich water flows.

Under what kind of conditions will you find a hydrothermal vent?
a. dark and hot
b. bright and cold
c. dry and windy
d. fertile and shady

Lava
(PAGES 10–11)
What magma is called when it reaches the outside of a volcano.

When are you likely to find lava in its hot, molten state?
a. during a tsunami
b. during an earthquake
c. during a volcanic eruption
d. during an aftershock

Magma
(PAGES 10–11)
Molten rock inside a volcano's vent, before it reaches the surface.

Where on Earth are you NOT likely to find magma?
a. at a hot spot
b. along the Ring of Fire
c. in a volcano vent
d. on top of a fault line

Molten
(PAGES 10–11)
Liquefied by heat, such as rock that is found beneath the Earth's surface.

In which layer of Earth would you find molten rock?
a. crust
b. mantle
c. inner core
d. outer core

Moment magnitude scale
(PAGES 34–35)
Developed by Thomas Hanks and Hiroo Kanamori, the moment magnitude scale measures the size of an earthquake by the amount of energy it releases.

Which is the best description for a 9.5 earthquake on the magnitude scale?
a. mild
b. average
c. strong
d. disastrous

Seismograph
(PAGES 34–35)
An instrument that detects small movements in Earth's crust.

Where do seismograph signals come from?
a. hurricanes
b. tsunamis
c. earthquakes
d. volcanoes

Tectonic plate
(PAGES 10–11, 18–19)
One of the many plates that make up the Earth's crust, each one able to shift and move.

Where is the most tectonic plate movement on Earth?
a. Mid-Atlantic Ridge
b. Ring of Fire
c. Hawaiian Islands
d. Mount St. Helens

Tsunami
(PAGES 16–17)
A large wave caused by earthquakes or large volcanic eruptions under the ocean.

Why are tsunamis dangerous to humans?
a. They move fast.
b. They carry tons of debris.
c. They flood coastal cities.
d. All of the above.

ANSWERS: caldera: **b.** composite volcano: **a.** dormant volcano: **d.** fissure: **c.** geothermal energy: **b.** hydrothermal vent: **a.** lava: **c.** magma: **d.** molten: **d.** moment magnitude scale: **d.** seismograph: **c.** tectonic plate: **b.** tsunami: **d**

FIND OUT MORE

BOOKS

Jump Into Science: Earthquakes
BY ELLEN J. PRAGER
National Geographic, 2007

National Geographic Readers: Volcanoes
BY ANNE SCHREIBER
National Geographic, 2008

National Geographic Science Chapters: Rivers of Fire: The Story of Volcanoes
BY MONICA HELPERN
National Geographic, 2006

Witness to Disaster: Earthquakes
BY JUDY FRADIN AND DENNIS FRADIN
National Geographic, 2008

Witness to Disaster: Volcanoes
BY JUDY FRADIN AND DENNIS FRADIN
National Geographic, 2007

FILMS TO WATCH

Doomsday Volcano
National Geographic, 2007

L.A.'s Future Quake
National Geographic, 2006

Man vs. Volcano
National Geographic, 2011

National Geographic Classics: Forces of Nature
National Geographic, 2010

Violent Earth
National Geographic, 2006

WEBSITES

U.S. Geological Survey: Earthquakes for Kids
earthquake.usgs.gov/learn/kids/

U.S. Geological Survey: Volcano Hazards Program
volcanoes.usgs.gov/

Weather Wiz Kids: Volcanoes
www.weatherwizkids.com/weather-volcano.htm

Weather Wiz Kids: Earthquakes
www.weatherwizkids.com/weather-earthquake.htm

Volcanoes: Earth's fiery power
www.nationalgeographic.com/environment/natural-disasters/volcanoes/

PLACES TO VISIT

Arenal National Park, Costa Rica
Bromo-Tengger-Semeru National Park, East Java, Indonesia
Iceland
Kilauea Volcano, Hawaii, U.S.A.
Mount Fuji, Japan
Mount Pacaya, Guatemala
Mount St. Helens, Washington State, U.S.A.
Our Dynamic Earth, Edinburgh, U.K.
Vesuvius National Park, Italy
Yellowstone National Park, Idaho, Montana, and Wyoming, U.S.A.

BOLDFACE INDICATES ILLUSTRATIONS.

A

Acid lakes 27, **27**
Animals
    earthquake prediction and 36, 37
    search and rescue 56, **56–57**
Arenal Volcano, Costa Rica **30**
Ash clouds **26–27**, 47, 50, **58–59**
Atlantis (legendary city) 48, **48–49**, 49
Avalanches 16, **16–17**

B

Bacteria 24
Basalt columns **30**
Black smokers 25, **25**
Blue Lagoon, Iceland **28–29**

C

Calderas 13, 23, **31**, 48, 61
Chickens 37, **37**
Chile
    earthquakes 11, 41
    volcano **23**
Christchurch, New Zealand: quake damage 17
Cinder cone volcanoes 23, **23**, **51**
Cockroaches 56, **56**
Composite volcanoes 23, **23**, **51**, 61
Crater Lake, U.S.A. 23, **23**

D

Danakil Depression, Ethiopia **30**
Diamonds 29, **29**
Djibouti: volcanic cones **30**
Dome volcanoes 23, **23**, **51**
Dormant volcanoes 26, 61

E

Earth (planet)
    axis 41
    geothermal features 12
    layers 8, 13, **13**, 53, **53**
    photo gallery **30–31**
    see also Tectonic plates
Earthquake simulators 40, **40**
Earthquakes
    aftershocks 11, 14, 17, 39
    energy release 43
    magnitude scale 35, 50, 61
    prediction 13, 34, 36, 37
    seismic waves 34, 35

El Chichón (volcano), Mexico **19**
Elephants 36, **36–37**
Etna, Mount (volcano), Sicily, Italy **20–21**, **31**, 52, **52**
Eyjafjallajökull (volcano), Iceland **26–27**, **58–59**

F

Fault lines 11, 15, 39
Films: volcanoes and earthquakes 52–53
Fimmvorouhals (volcano), Iceland 30
Fissures 22, **22**, 61
Fumaroles 12

G

Gabbro 51, **51**
Geothermal energy 28, 61
Geysers 12, 13, **13**
Giant's Causeway, Northern Ireland 30
Glass, volcanic 51, **51**
Granite porphyry 51, **51**
Great Rift Valley, Africa **30**
Greek mythology 49

H

Hanks, Thomas 35, 61
Hawaii
    lava flow **4–5**
    legend 46
    volcanoes 23, 47, 60, 64
Hawaiian Islands: formation 23
Hood, Mount (volcano), U.S.A. **31**
Hot springs 12, 13, 25, 28
Hydrothermal vents 24, 25, **25**, 61

I

Iceland
    geothermal energy 28
    lagoon **28–29**
    volcanoes **26–27**, 30, 47, **58–59**
Igneous rocks 51, **51**
Indonesia
    mudflow **17**
    volcanoes **18**, 27, 27, 42, **44–45**
Iron 13, 51, 53

J

Japan
    earthquakes 16, 32, 39, 56, 64
    hot springs 28
    tsunamis **2–3**, 16, 56, 64

K

Kaula-Kona, Hawaii **4–5**
Kamchatka Peninsula, Russia **31**
Kanamori, Hiro 35, 61
Karymsky (volcano), Russia **10**
Kilauea (volcano), Hawaii 46, **60**, 64
Kimberlite 29
Krakatau (volcano), Indonesia **18**, 42

L

Lava: definition 10, 61
Lava caves 27, **27**
Lava domes 14, 23, **23**, **51**
Lava flows 4–5, 7, 10, **20–21**, 27, **30**
Lava fountains **31**, 47
Lava lakes 7, **54–55**
Lava lamp: how to make 47, **47**
Legends 46, 48
Licancabur (volcano), Chile **23**
Lightning **26–27**, 27

M

Magma: definition 10, 61
Magma chambers 22, **22**, 23, 61
Map 18–19
Mars (planet): volcano 25
Mauna Loa (volcano), Hawaii **23**, 47
Merapi, Mount, Indonesia: mudflow **17**
Mexico City, Mexico: quake-proof building **41**
Mid-ocean ridges 25
Mineral spas 28, **29**
Miyako, Japan: tsunami **2–3**, 64
Moment magnitude scale 35, 50, 61
Mountain ranges 13, 25, 49
Mud baths 28, **29**
Mud pots **10**, 12
Mudflows 17, **17**, 51
Myanmar: quake damage **1**, 64

N

New Zealand
    spas 29, **29**
    volcanoes 52, **52**
    see also Christchurch
Ngauruhoe (volcano), New Zealand 52, **52**
Nickel 13, 53
Nyiragongo (volcano), Congo 54, **54–55**
Nyos, Lake, Cameroon 27

O

Obsidian 51, **51**
Ol Doinyo Lengai (volcano), Tanzania **6–7**
Old Faithful (geyser), U.S.A. 13
Osaka, Japan: quake damage **32–33**

P

Pakistan (earthquake) 14
Pele (deity) 46, **46**
Pelée, Mount (volcano), Martinique 37
Pik Kommunizma, Tajikistan **16–17**
Pinatubo, Mount (volcano), Philippines **18**
Pit vipers 37, **37**
Plato 48, **48**
Plutonic rocks 51, **51**
Pompeii, Italy 15, **15**
Port-au-Prince, Haiti 14, **14**, **31**
Power plant, geothermal **28–29**
Pumice 29, **29**, 51, 51
Puy de Dôme (volcano) France **23**

R

Redwoods 38, **38**
Rescue work 40, **40**, 56, **56–57**
Ring of Fire: illustrated diagram **18–19**
Rocks, volcanic 29, 51, **51**

S

San Andreas Fault, U.S.A. 38, **38**
San Francisco, U.S.A. 14, **14**, 36, 38, 40
Seafloor spreading 25
Search and rescue dogs 56, **56–57**
Seiches 39

Seismographs 35, **35**, 61
Seismometer, ancient 35
Shield volcanoes 23, **23**, **51**
Snow monkeys 28
Snowdon, Mount (volcano) U.K. 53
Soil 13, 28
St. Helens, Mount (volcano), U.S.A. **19**, 27
Stratovolcanoes. *see* Composite volcanoes
Submersible **24**
Sulphur 25, 26

T

Tambora, Mount (volcano), Indonesia **18**, 27, 27
Tectonic plates 11, 13, 23, 43, 49, 61
    diagram **11**
    map 18–19
Tofua Island, Tonga 31
Toxic gases 26, 54
Tsunamis **2–3**, 16–17, 36, 39, 43, **43**, 56, 61, 64
Tube worms 24, **24**

V

Vesuvius, Mount (volcano), Italy 15
Volcanic Explosivity Index (VEI) 50
Volcanoes
    diagram **22**
    hot spots 23
    island formation 7, 12, 23
    rating scale 50
    types of 23, **23**, **51**, **51**
    underwater 7, 24, 25
Volcanoes National Park, Rwanda 13
Volcanologists **20–21**, 26, **26**, 54, **54**
Vulcan (deity) 46, **46**

W

Washington, D.C., U.S.A.: earthquake 15, 52
Wave machine 39, **39**
Waves, giant. *see* Tsunamis

Y

Yellowstone National Park, U.S.A. 12, 13, **13**

Published by the National Geographic Society
John M. Fahey, Jr., *Chairman of the Board
and Chief Executive Officer*
Declan Moore, *Executive Vice President; President, Publishing
and Travel*
Melina Gerosa Bellows, *Executive Vice President;
Chief Creative Officer, Books, Kids, and Family*

Prepared by the Book Division
Hector Sierra, *Senior Vice President and General Manager*
Nancy Laties Feresten, *Senior Vice President,
Kids Publishing and Media*
Jay Sumner, *Director of Photography, Children's Publishing*
Jennifer Emmett, *Vice President, Editorial Director, Children's
Books*
Eva Absher-Schantz, *Design Director, Kids Publishing and Media*
R. Gary Colb t, *Production Director*
Jennifer A. Thornton, *Director of Managing Editorial*

Staff for This Book
Lynn Addison, Robin Terry, *Project Editors*
James Hiscott, Jr., *Art Director*
Annette Kiesow, *Illustrations Editor*
Joanna Wojtkowiak, *Designer*
Marisa Larson, *Researcher*
Callie Broaddus, *Design Production Assistant*
Hillary Moloney, *Associate Photo Editor*
Carl Mehler, *Director of Maps*
Matt Chwastyk, *Map Research and Production*
Grace Hill, *Associate Managing Editor*
Joan Gossett, *Production Editor*
Lewis R. Bassford, *Production Manager*
Susan Borke, *Legal and Business Affairs*

Production Services
Phillip L. Schlosser, *Senior Vice President*
Chris Brown, *Vice President, NG Book Manufacturing*
George Bounelis, *Vice President, Production Services*
Nicole Elliott, *Manager*
Rachel Faulise, *Manager*
Robert L. Barr, *Manager*

Captions
Cover: Kilauea on the Big Island of Hawaii is one of the world's most active volcanoes. The word Kilauea means 'spewing' in the Hawaiian language.
Page 1: This giant crack in a roadway in Tarlay, Shan State, in northeastern Myanmar, was caused by a 6.8 magnitude earthquake, which knocked down 130 houses in the same area.
Pages 2–3: A tsunami, which followed a 9.0 magnitude earthquake, caused water to flow into the city of Miyako, Iwate, Japan, in March 2011.
Back cover: Molten lava flowing. Hawaii, U.S.A.

Published by Collins
An imprint of HarperCollins Publishers
Westerhill Road
Bishopbriggs
Glasgow G64 2QT
www.harpercollins.co.uk

HarperCollins Publishers
1st Floor, Watermarque Building, Ringsend Road, Dublin 4, Ireland

In association with National Geographic Partners, LLC

NATIONAL GEOGRAPHIC and the Yellow Border Design are trademarks of the National Geographic Society, used under license.

Second edition 2018
First published 2013

ISBN 978-0-00-826781-0

10 9 8 7 6

The contents of this publication are believed correct at the time of printing. Nevertheless the publisher can accept no responsibility for errors or omissions, changes in the detail given or for any expense or loss thereby caused.

HarperCollins does not warrant that any website mentioned in this title will be provided uninterrupted, that any website will be error free, that defects will be corrected, or that the website or the server that makes it available are free of viruses or bugs. For full terms and conditions please refer to the site terms provided on the website.

A catalogue record for this book is available from the British Library

Printed in Great Britain by Bell & Bain Ltd, Glasgow

If you would like to comment on any aspect of this book, please contact us at the above address or online.
natgeokidsbooks.co.uk
collins.reference@harpercollins.co.uk

Paper from responsible sources

Since 1888, the National Geographic Society has funded more than 12,000 research, exploration, and preservation projects around the world. The Society receives funds from National Geographic Partners, LLC, funded in part by your purchase. A portion of the proceeds from this book supports this vital work. To learn more, visit natgeo.com/info.